TRANSLATION ZONE

T0168865

Translation Zone

Poems

Brian Cochran

MARSH HAWK PRESS • 2023
East Rockaway, New York

Marsh Hawk books are published by Marsh Hawk Press, Inc.,
a not-for-profit corporation under section 501(c)3
United States Internal Revenue Code.

Cover design: Kevin Cochran • Cover art: Sai Li
Book design & typesetting: Mark Melnick

FIRST EDITION
Library of Congress Cataloging-in-Publication Data

Names: Cochran, Brian, author.
Title: Translation zone / Brian Cochran.
Other titles: Translation zone (Compilation)
Description: First edition. | East Rockaway : Marsh Hawk Press, 2023.
Identifiers: LCCN 2022046339 | ISBN 9780998658254 (paperback)
Subjects: LCGFT: Poetry.
Classification: LCC PS3553.O2477 T73 2023 | DDC 811/.54--dc23/eng/20221117
LC record available at https://lccn.loc.gov/2022046339

Publication of this title was made possible in part by a regrant awarded
and administered by the Community of Literary Magazines and Presses (CLMP).
CLMP's NYS regrant programs are made possible by the New York State Council on
the Arts with the support of Governor Kathy Hochul and the New York State Legislature.

Marsh Hawk Press
P.O. Box 206, East Rockaway, N.Y. 11518-0206
mheditor@marshhawkpress.org

Contents

For

Mary Jane Cochran
(JUNE 22, 1925 – NOVEMBER 16, 2018)

George H. Cochran
(SEPTEMBER 23, 1913 – OCTOBER 1, 2008)

Translation Zone

At what we call *the confluence*, the way people talk about their relationship, as if there is no other, waters collide to form a kind of wall. The relatively swift Missouri collides with the slow, deep Mississippi, and you can see a vague line where it's happening, a dreamed transitional space, a location for analysts or poets to inhabit, though some prefer paragraphs or other measures.

The river's mouth is where my friend goes for language. The Missouri is an exceptionally roiled and muddy river; it's hard not to imagine the words being dirty there. My friend, one of the steadiest people I have ever known, is unperturbed. Bring me your dirt and radiation, your unborn flowers, enormous snags, bring it all, he seems to say.

The poem too is a kind of transitional space, the poem is de-aspirational in its marketing stance, and as a space, does not prefer things in bins, or shrink-wrapped in plastic, or internet delivered. It has its preferences, but they are not in packaging or means of distribution, not really, though you might hardly know that for all the talk of formatting.

Urban life is often reduced to the notion of the "container," like the containers used for storing and shipping merchandize. The city: a container of containers, writes Sergio González Rodríguez, speaking of Ciudad Juárez. Walls are safety zones, areas of exclusion, although I just misread that as wars are safety zones, areas of exclusion.

Writer-translator Yoko Tawada believes that words are not containers of meaning so much as they are gates that open onto the chasm into which all languages fall. A gate involves a border, a translation zone, a threshold. The Middle English *ook*, for oak, is also, in druidic usage, the root word for door. This is, I think, what Tawada is saying.

The wall formed by the collision of rivers, where the water of one meets the other and doesn't flow right or left, not really, just into, on, through, is one I have seen a deer practically walk across. The deer was in the water on the far side of the Missouri, being swept downstream. I was almost afraid to watch. When she hit the water wall, she calmly turned and used it, swimming almost without effort along the translation zone.

Hummingbird Migration

The migration of these tiny birds, each weighing about the same as the nickel in your pocket, can only be described as *massive*, an odd word to use for anything as small as a hummingbird. But in the story people want to buy, which is mostly what we're talking about when we talk about stories, I'm standing on a drilling platform eighty-four miles out in the gulf, when the air fills with nickels whizzing by.

I don't know why we say *the air fills*, but in the literature, as in life, hummingbird migration is a figure for the borders we keep, nickels going south, nickels as the secret Swiss bank accounts of boys and girls in un-numbered pockets, nickels beautiful as hummingbirds, and currency a coin that has value *today*, to people, as in we *the* people, boys and girls of the United States.

Some books will tell you migration is only temporary, but there they are talking about birds, not nickels or thinking. And with nickels seem to go our onto-mono-theological presumptions (to quote a coinage of Fred Moten's), another kind of currency, but one we send as *just stuff*, to people we refuse to believe are living inside a different kind of book.

The truth is that hummingbird migration can only be described as *singular*, since each bird travels utterly alone. The 5-gram comparison with the nickel is about right though, since hummers roughly double their weight before the gulf crossing, then burn it off during the flight. So they leave as nickels, arrive as dimes.

The arts, popular and commercial, and the artier ones too, have taken advantage of how hummingbird migration opens borders, making them increasingly ductile and fluid, which is why so many are working with notions of liminal space, seams, in-between zones.

Though it seems that, like Orpheus, artists have always passed through mirrors or gates, crossed rivers or entered images to inhabit other zones.

Every hummingbird is born with its own map and schedule for migration; each fledgling is driven out of the mother's territory as soon as she has taught it to feed. The first journey to the south is then made alone, but the time and direction for it are known, inside the hummingbird, just as certain mystical traditions know that meaning is a given, that life begins in a moment of absolute knowledge, and our itineraries are not *towards* meaning, but proceeding *from* it. Which explains a lot about how we can become so lost.

Beneath the graphs and thinkings of hummingbird migration theory, there is always the simple desire for a beautiful or funny story, a sign like the gates of a drilling rig festooned with ruby throats, a moment like the chaste orgasm at the intersection of supply and demand curves, a time as alive as the dream-swarms buzzing past on invisible currents, as funny as the two roughnecks outside on break, shaking their heads, saying dude we shouldn't have smoked that stuff.

But the truth is that the two or three grams of creature skimming the waves alone, sometimes dipping down in the troughs, mostly invisible, at heights of six or nine feet, a true insanity of nature, is enough. Beyond the currency of our wishes.

In the odd connections and disconnections between our words and actions, the medium of exchange is mostly desire. The making and breaking point of what goes on between us, though this seems most visible in childhood. Flying from knowledge into mystery, the hummingbirds between us know what they know, though we are only their tiniest meanings.

Egrets, Regrets

To look at Gogol's overcoat and see how the coat itself becomes the main character in the tale, the way the poor clerk disappears beneath the weights of value—social, personal, survival—invested in a thing, is to see form. Not as shape or outline, but a kind of immanence. The way feelings that are formless seek to attach to people dreams words theories acts to exist in a material word that form lies trapped in.

No doubt my poetry errs, wrote Hopkins, *but as air* . . . .

Air and err and air and err. A kind of sonic opening.

My regrets bend back their long necks to pick at the scapulars.

In the Marxist reading of Bartleby, the lawyer's indifference becomes the main character in the tale. This feels like an allegory of form. In air.

To speak of the parable in parabola is to sing a little. Which isn't on the agenda today.

Gogol's mistranslated overcoat is really the cloak of social concerns.

How difficult to put something out there.

formal poem

the prepositional phrase over and over roils the mind like a wave
razed beach the waves the very ones she removes to find the thing
the rose is looking for the girl who is nine the one with the eyebrows
and thatch of hair the one who holds the lostness of small places a
certain way to remove the primary wave till valence till current till
what the they the the the the bird call calls wave form occurs in the
lonely paint drip *that* wave form, *that*

Placement of the No's

In Noh, the actors wear masks so something else can be seen.
Expression comes from the underside of the mask. A good mask
requires no padding. Lamentations 2 exhorts us not to mask our
tears. A stanza is a kind of mask; a stance is a way of standing

right justified

in a line, a kind of informal misunderstanding. The line break
is a kind of lie. A politician is a mask in which the underside
has no expression. The pretense of feeling allows great freedom
of representation. Washing one's hands can make what is

written

more difficult to read. A face with tears is a changed mask.
The ancestral is always present in mask making. At this
point, the temptation to copy may become too great. Those
who do not participate in a system of trust may not

believe

in its language. The good mask requires no padding to fit
the actor's face. In Noh, the actors wear masks so something
else can be seen. Expression comes from the underside
of the mask. Most important is the placement of

the nose

ideas tuned, not music

crushed trumpet blossoms on the stairs
soft memos to the supply side
of economic theory
the poem's
mean

ing

to

out

line

each
dream

flower

in

chalk

evidence for the detectives
of crushed blossoms always underfoot
how each petal hit chance lit moment
takes in the rain, the hard slant of rain
hard and slanted, I said, rain,
whatever instrument this is
let it play

Preliminary Remarks With
Love Poem & Marriage Proposal

But what I do not wish to talk about tonight is the maquiladora of the social heart. Maquila being the assembly industry. The social heart assembling all that is *appropriate* and *good* so peerlessly the city of El Paso exists as the perfect double of the Ciudad Juárez we are standing in tonight. And what we are talking about here is Philip Guston's late work, specifically *Couple in Bed*, 1977, 81 × 94.5, courtesy of the McKee Gallery, the bristly pipe-cleaner legs and clip-clop shoes, brushes grasped as if clutching a heart, the couple so close, so closed, like strangers on a rush hour train in Tokyo.

According to myths from the north, the maquiladoras rained down from the sky, and that's true, if by *sky* we mean the theories and thinkings of political economy. Where they reside, in reference to the city. *Ach-too!* [spitting sound] Excuse me, the dust in my teeth.

The maquiladora and its assemblage are so pervasive that Ciudad Juárez resembles nothing so much as an enormous collage. The assemblage industry inscribed on the heart of the city, the assemblage art thereby reproduced across the living sprawl like a kind of garbage burning in the trenches of words. Things have a way of replicating themselves, given the limited number of known forms.

The sky and the busy old fool that rises there every day has been around awhile, but the dust tastes different, almost metallic now. And the maquiladora, like the social heart that obscures it, the El Pasos we use as buffers against it, can be employed as surely as a rose or branch of flowers to disarm a lover. Intoxicated by this irony, the poet fills the deep hole of the poem's rectangle with the maquiladora's figure, as if the maquila were what holds and keeps us. Which we've already seen is true.

To say the same thing a different way: how tiresome to cut the pornography into small rectangles, then reassemble it, glued to the page, as a beautiful flesh-colored wave hovering over shadow, an expansive, not reductive, form. Given the limited number of known forms.

If I am the slow accretion of many brush strokes, if I am the projection of form into deep space, and by "I" I mean the allegorical pronoun, not me standing here, if I am these things, then the image of the maquiladora should be understood as an allegory for the offshored, outsourced soul.

On the border here, I ask you where the lines are between things that have never existed before they exist. The s/he-art and its subjects, where are they made? By whose hand? In what marriage? Let us bear these questions in mind as we enter our workshop on the subjective today.

Crushed On Trumpet Blossom Stairs

the blossom i call trumpet for
        the sound drawn in wax   the seeing eye
needle
        taps the *hill and dale* groove in yeah
wax
   for that
               blind man   yeah
    his synesthesiastic
  tap
         in topographic groove
fuck yeah   yeah
   for that for   whitmans
newsmans tap for
             snyders
rip rap tack-
       hammer tap
          i hear the crying world here the
                  trumpet sax bass
     the front stairs a keyboard
   some
               monk could play
the crushed trumpet blossoms pressed   under foot
         on the landing [*there*]
          as in a book
  of migratory
     stairs   yeah
  take that
       shake

to rearrange   into
         some
            deaf
         hexameter
    goes like this:
the crushed on trumpet blossom stairs

Mourning, "Morning," I say.

Things have a way of unfolding along their creases: tears trace a hard crease, almost a fissure, there.

In the Lament for Ur, in xxx b.c., we see unironic longing, the first being the earliest known writing in what later became the elegiac tradition, the second the poet's initials following kiss markings. ~~North and written to be sung in the voice of the city's goddess~~. The crossed out makes a dark sound.

Tears can feel torn. This occurs particularly when there is a mask involved. What is torn then is the mask, still worn and loved, and therefore the face and mind. The terror involved in this need only be mentioned to be understood.

The flow of tears involves the same principles of fluid dynamics and gravity as the flow of rivers. All dynamics are fluid. There is an odd relationship between the sounds of grief and singing, crying and laughing.

As all rivers have slope, all emotions have gravity in the world. In the steady stream of the real.

Mourning, "Morning," I say.

Invention of Non-Mechanical[1] Trephination

man with crucifix belt and only words to stand on
realizing (!) that self-trephining is really stupid!
In laughing at this/himself,[2] he is cured.

Trephination (tre-fə-'nā-shən) *n.* [from the Greek *trypanon*, auger; also *trupan*, to bore] surgical process of drilling a hole in the skull. According to John Verano, professor of anthropology at Tulane University, trephination is the oldest known surgical practice, based on archaeological evidence in the form of cave paintings and trephined human remains. A trephined skull found in France was dated to 5,000 BCE. Many trephined skulls unearthed at various sites show signs of healing and indicate that the patient lived for years after the event, even sometimes having trephination performed again later in life, and again surviving the event. Bart Huges (b. 1934), a medical school graduate who never practiced medicine except for a bit of self-surgery, believed that trephination is the way to higher consciousness. He wanted to be a psychiatrist but failed the obstetrics exam and so never went into practice. In 1965, after years of experimentation with LSD, cannabis, and other drugs, Dr. Huges realized that the way to enlightenment was by boring a hole in his skull. He used an electric drill, a scalpel, and a hypodermic needle (to administer a local anesthetic). The operation took him 45 minutes. How did it feel to be enlightened? "I feel like I did when I was 14," said Huges.

[1] Here, non-mechanical means based on understanding. Understanding refers to mind | body | heart (,) taken as a whole, though in various orders. It is always out loud, even when silent. The phenomenon is momentary, though its reverberations are deep reaching and may last a very long time. This is what is meant by "changing the world". Understanding, as a medical intervention, is not "treating", so much as it is changing what is. Also see [3]

[2] Early references to non-mechanical trephination were made by the author's father, who, upon achieving something, habitually made the wry comment that now all of his problems were solved, except for the holes in his head. The wryness and humor of this are the non-mechanical part. The overall context suggests the unsatisfactoriness of achievement as a solution, the humor suggests the nascent awareness of a non-mechanical solution, the holes the need for some form of trephination, or perhaps for healing.

[3] Under standing literally means being in the ground, grounded, standing under what is,[4] not on top of it. The preferred form of lovemaking for one who believes in this may well not be "on top," but held "down" by the be-lover. I love your reality, s/he is saying, I am blessed and in joy to be its witness (s/he being the one held in this manner). The preferred form of lovemaking for one who believes in this may also be on "top". In this s/he is saying, I am grounded by you; you are my ground, I love my reality on your ground, as I try to love it elsewhere, and I love you to bear witness to it, here, with me. It should be understood that either situation is a rare state to attain in love, and should be treated as sacred, though to do so may undermine or prevent it. This is the human condition.

[4] In this connection, under standing should also be understood as the locus of the soul. cf: Notley, Alice; *The Descent of Alette*: ". . .your soul" "Which is" "what you are" "below the ground"

Terms of Resurrection

cornell, joseph/ heteroclitic assemblage artist/ b. 1903−d./
in 5 days/ age 69/ all head/ no body/ sunflower withered/
on its stalk/ a face/ the eternal/ age of shock/ resurrection
ist/ detritus sifter/ un-surreal/ lover/ of the lost/ of the un
sexually/ erotic/ perfection/ of placement/ accumulation/
of the numinous/ in a world/ of souvenir/ oh star spools/
lost threads/ of tenderness/ oh cornell joseph/ heteroclitic
assemblage artist/ b. 1903−d./ in 5 days/ at 69/ only then
/from stellar clouds/ for 25,167 lost and bodyless days/ it
fell/ the gentle storm/ of erotic dust/ charged as all things
/ armies, lovers, lyrical intensities/ that turn/ to you/ you
being dust/ my fellow celibate/ fantasist/ unwiller to live/
with the terms of what is

Asking the Dust

I ask my old consultants, and they say just follow. Me, us. That was
before it started to rain. I follow the motes, thinking of Flaubert,
how he labored months to find that oh, je ne sais quoi, right mote.
Pardon the dust humor. But think of how he is read now, mostly in
translation, which is to say *in other words*, literally in other words, the
joke being on him, that there is no right mote, dust being a collective
phenomenon, seeking a single horizon to translate down to the
ground.

Out in the driveway, a slicker-coated kid is working the puddles
with a little trenching shovel. He imagines himself canal builder,
waterway designer, and of course president, since it's, what, 1962? My
friend reads a poem in her childhood bedroom, the poem is mine, the
experience hers, in the streams the kid is making in the driveway, in
the moats of muddied water, there is no right,
                    just this
left
word. But there we flirt with the flattened plane, the belief in dust
being its own lover, always finding a ground, the erotics of that gentle
sifting, after a dying.

What Philip Guston painted toward the end was the way an object
is itself, picked up and placed in a different constellation. The dust
won't leave us, being in love with its own tiny voices, the right motes,
a single horizon, the inter-subjective ways we are found alone.

A muddy, gritty, tender thing to hold.

Werewolf Dreams

Whenever I dream of werewolves, I am always aware of exactly where my body is in the real world, and when my eyes open, the transition between the inwardly dreamt and outwardly seen is seamless, so precise is the mapping. The only difference is the werewolf disappears. Always. This has led me to believe that werewolves can only exist, really, in the transitional spaces between things, between dreams and waking, figure and ground, in the feelings between the named feelings, the moments when we are between ourselves.

Sometimes I think that the writer or artist is nothing so much as a weir creature, and at least in the instant between the dreamed topography and its map appearing on a canvas or paper or screen, there is a transformation.

The last time I dreamed of a werewolf, he looked a lot like Jack Spicer, only taller, standing at the foot of the bed with a kindly, avuncular expression on his face, silver glasses hanging low off the hairy nose. That's when I tried to kick him as hard as I've ever tried to kick anything in my life, because, you know, he was *a werewolf.*

Then, with my hamstring tearing in slow motion, somewhere inside the bright shock of injury a ripcord pulled to stop the story from unfurling, as real as the echo of my own scream, a thousand miles from the other side of the dream.

So this is where I crawled to the light switch across the floor, this is where I slowly put on clothes, hobbled to the drugstore to buy a cane, then caught the flight to New Haven to hear Alice Notley read, found her in the basement where she would later speak. This is what I have, the story I've briefly told.

But there is no story in the dream measure the poem takes of things, where it is now thinking of another place, just off the hallway, in a bedroom with blue stars, as a child in a crib has his first memory, the light coming under the door-crack, the shadow of someone loved and familiar passing down the hall.

Plains

where does wind originate

      but a library in paterson

          aeolus in brooklyn

             the wind blown diction of the platte

       in logaoedic buffalo grass its

four foot roots

       in a vastness of dust once

           alluvial then
aeolian

        sediment, loess

    below the three-inch tufts

        what I meant to say is

      the wind from the books ruffles the bluestem prairie of my
father's hair

bridgeward

along the Mississippi, cold
or

                     cold   &

           eagles,   sustained   black   dots   in the tree line

(the the-ness of the, the revisedness of revision) their

            impossibly muscled   planked wings

               broad, paved as a road

    over
              ice-choked

underflow

L'Adieu La Dieu

Over the radio, a voice says *the bird sings with its fingers*. L'oiseau chante avec ses doigts. Odd to hear the same quality of assonance fall across the two languages, one meaning. Sings and fingers; chante | avec ses doigts. Petals on a dark, black bough.

Orphée is taking dictation from the internet of his day. Apollinaire, murdered by the inner structures of fascism we carry around inside because we were children once, is writing a blog. What does it mean to die?

It means listening over airwaves to the living, though perhaps murdered by the inner structures of fascism, as they intone from another world, outside the medieval gates.

It means what the academic poets wrote in the fifties, then, horrified, turned to a line-broken religion of typographic notation as codified by Olson while falling off his own personal cliff.

Dying also means taking dictation from the Apollinaires of your day, staying technically alive due to continual downloads of each new poetic operating system. After all, this is the model established across the sixties, no no no never again that embarrassment, in this material word, I mean world, of being caught inside an archaic religion or in fact believing in . . . well, anything. Except currency. Its cool coinage.

Of course to live in the Salon of the Refused before it has even been invented may feel like its own kind death.

Yet Orpheus to me Orphée to Cocteau is a great artist, simply one who's dying inside the academy, that garage where the vehicle and its transmission, of the once beautiful, now dead, messaging theologies, occurs.

L'oiseau chante avec ses doigts. Deux fois.

And what of the vitriers lugging their weirs through the wind tousled streets of the zone? The great library at alexandria is always burning to the ground, the vitriers peddling views into what was and is left of it. Every window has traveled half way to being a mirror.

L'oiseau chante avec ses doigts. Trois fois.

The real autobiography of this ex mirror salesman involves loss from breakage, scaffolding built inside the station wagon in a vain attempt to stem the breakage, then scaffolding built to sustain the something-that-is despite the breakage, and so on. A working title is *The Theology of Mirror Vendors*.

There is always the risk of becoming a mere vendor, but *poïesis*, according to Wikipedia, reconciles thought with matter and time, person with world.

L'Adieu is a poem by Apollinaire. La Dieu is the female god. I wait for you, remember.

Location, Location, Location

A man said she sang beyond the genius of the sea.
I would say this too!
but I am in Nebraska
with Whitman and Williams
the voice of Crane by the cranes
and you are where the great unplains begin,
with Stevens.

siblings, prepositions

the of of of

odd between its others

only the middle one functional

identical genes, which here I think means letters

what is that compared to the syntax of living

that   of

An Introduction to the *Field Guide* *of North American Lycanthropy*

Sometimes the wise of a thing is impenetrable. Though if you look closely at its face, you'll see a kindly, avuncular expression there, the wry humor, the curiosity towards an other, asleep in a life or waking or somewhere in between. All things are like this in the face. Look. You'll notice how they inhabit us in places where we would prefer to sleep. Just as certain birds are found only in riparian woodlands, others in ravines, just as golden eagles know their terrain as air current, and never stoop to feed in areas of persistent downdraft, some things can only exist in the spaces between things, the zone where Missouri meets Mississippi, in the river under the river, the place they call Itasca from which an old collage of seepages and springs is given a name, perceived as whole. This is change, a kind of waking. When Amar Kanwar talks of a border, he imagines the line running extremely deep and high. The poetic line often lies, like this, inside another form. All containers are meaning. In France, in 1890, when the workers on the line in the factory for wooden shoes called *sabots*, taking the product in hand, invented *sabotage*, we see how language is made. Wear it well on your travels, my friend, this mask, this other, these whys.

[to say dehiscence]

to say *dehiscence*
after reading it, looking
it up

> the calla lilies rioting across the privilege line

1. the natural opening up of the anther or other flower part to
   bloom

2. the bursting open of a surgically closed wound

> there, to hear its double music

"the dehiscence
of Afro American studies
in the university"

> in the originating text

hands

fold a piece of paper into a crane: the sentence   as cultural reference
    deftly folds
                    its unsaid
  origami
                            and likely unseen unheard
    gru canadensis
                        into the neat phrase

        like a cleaned out room

    emptied of the great conflagration of sandhill cranes in nebraska
    in march

emptied of the *in*   with its dense cultural references
                    [i long to hold you in]
references   to the things contained   in state, month, side

                        in the space between
            my separating membrane
            and the world you are in
                                    the space of experience
        the sentence unfolds out into

        like a player folding his hand

    in a time and space when merwin was still opening his
                    book circa whenever that was
to now

—*for Lee K. Abbott*

The Sound of Meaning

The man pulling and turning
the boats, *scrip* of scrape on sand
hrmp of heave,
gnnn of aluminum,
his pained look that says
hangover to me today,
which is to say
in my memory now
he is hung over
from drinking that night
by the river I dipped my foot in
again and again
when I was ten,
always the same act
always different,
as the poem which has fur now
is a dying cicada
come back to life later
and before that a frog
someone tries to stomp on,
the mind being its own place:
let me show you how
this is *water*
　　水
and this *sound*
　　の音
and this the *sound of water*
　　水 の 音
or at least pictures of things that mean
the sound of water

as Ginsberg who died in 1997 and is gone
translates
in that famous moment from Bashō
who died in 1694
kerplunk

Architecture

It is the volume you hold
not the one you write
or turn up. The space
between objects, people,
not the objects or people.

It is the volume in that space,
the structure of things it makes around it.
But no no no (how easy the shift to figure
from terrible ground) it is the space
itself, like the air held by the room
so you can heat or cool it.

It is the place we really inhabit.
It is what's gone after
the building is gone.
Then a different kind of space
everywhere on the skyline.

Romance Sonámbulo

I first heard the opening line of Lorca's famous poem while interviewing the poet and novelist Julia Alvarez in 1998. "I love Lorca. You know, *verde que te quiero verde*," she said, "Green, I love you green." I didn't know, but did register her verde on my scale of sounds, its echoes with verdant and the French vert.

The word is an ironic notation of something ancient and difficult to approach, says the painter Francesco Clemente, speaking of *palimpsest*, though what he says resonates in the mind's ear for any word, really. The notion that a word, each word, is like a palimpsest, a parchment erased and rewritten upon again and again in the succeeding eras, days, moods, commercial and emotive needs that form a language.

I didn't read Lorca's poem until long after the Alvarez interview, but driving through my hometown in 2002, after a long absence, I realized that the green in Kent, Ohio was the right green, pinned to the day and season, as it was nowhere else in the world. In that moment, I remembered the thought-sound in Alvarez's voice when she said *verde*.

Then years later, when I finally stumbled across *Sonambular Ballad*, opening to it in a plain prose translation by J.L. Gili, what it held for me was mostly intense erotic longing. Though the green of home was also there.

The range of translations for the poem's simple first line is astonishing. Green, I love you, green. Green as I would have you green. Green, how much I want you green. Green here is an ironic notation of something ancient, a palimpsest for the laying on of hands, one hand on top of another, each successive pair of hands replacing the previous hands. What touch means. Green wind. Green skin. Green limbs.

Reading the poem out loud in a library room last month, I heard it whole for the first time. Green wind, writes Lorca, and the wind is blowing outside the window in New Hampshire. Long pine needles have begun to fall, carpeting last week's gravelly road home. Green limbs, he writes. The horse on the mountain and the house on the hill. There is a woman on a balcony. Green flesh. The shadow at her waist as if desire itself were green, lambent green. Something is watching her that she does not know. As the poem goes on, Lorca imagines his own death, the Spanish Civil Guard pounding on the door, as the woman's lover, mortally wounded, is trying to climb a distant hill. It is a death haunted as much as it is a desire inhabited poem.

When I read the poem these days, with my mother entering the last stages of her life, my frequent trips to Houston, her demands, longings, wishes, memories, I feel green mostly as an intense desire to live, to hold to life. Also the longing for Andalusia in memory, that green. The flicker that inhabits all living.

We are always sleepwalking through dreamed greens.

My father died on October 1, 2008. The way his breathing changed during the last two hours, climbing a distant hill. My astonishment at what hard work it is to die. The moment when life translated out of the body, no longer him, only body.

Some translations require a kind of erasure. Others require additional words, scrapings, rewritings, notes. My erased translation of the Lorca poem has needed both.

Hue, want hue, green.
Eyebrow riddled
green, green
wind,
  green
limns,
green comma green,
    the rose skin tree limb
green
the invisible thread my father soughs in its leaves
that green

Verde que te quiero green.

For All the List Poems We Wrote in Grad School

To love the victims of the criminal act
who then become its perpetrators.
To think, unlayer this.
To bear evidence of whatever that is
in every footnoted lyric
the poem calls as its witness
to sing, if it must
in the deaf hearing rooms, where
meaning is transcribed
and no one allowed to listen.
To let the form go, to neither
break nor inhabit its lines,
but live between doorways and corridors
bearing the invisible layers
as if it were only translation
that allows the poem to be
a child bride to truth,
and with due respect to the groom,
to never marry him.

Fragmentation

Take fragrance
its *frag*

in a different context
its meaning

as fragile
as anything we hold to

or not, insistently making it
it meaning meaning

but what I was getting to

was frag
the verb

from the sixties-seventies nexus
some of us grew up in

that difficult emotional state

the way we used *fuck* or *fucking* as little plosive
call-outs, sincerity markers, in every other sentence

the way a piece of shrapnel
might takes decades to work to the surface

the fragrance of cordite

the hummingbirds that exit the terrible flower
with their loud thrumming

the way *shrapnel* sounds out
the shrap of flight
the null-
ity of struck flesh

the fra
of brother, where
can it be?

it meaning meaning

Crepuscule With Whoah Nellie

In Thelonious Monk's tune *Crepuscule With Nellie*, the French
crepuscule alludes to a space of freedom black americans could find
in Paris in the fifties, in the mind. It is 1957. I am two. Miles Davis is
already who he is as a player, a hawk in juvenile plumage. Don't ask
me where the birds came from: they were here first. *Ornithology* is
a jazz standard by Charlie Parker. Bird song, in Donald Kroodsma's
view, is a kind of thick word. Like *mine*. Can you hear the second
syrinx chime in? All morning, the red-shouldered hawk calling above
the now-leafy, once just-brick subdivision, a difficult identification.
Irish clay miners, unskilled labor, once dug clay here with their
bare hands, some fearing another form of labor called *slave*. Brick
yards along the river. Field markings. St. Louis, another difficult
identification. Is child-birth a form of labor? What poem-thought
is not hybrid? In juvenile plumage. The way marks, in a painting, can
be a form of sound. Sometimes form or formal mean *stand in for*, as
in *form* of labor or *formal* poetry. In the title of the tune, *Nellie* is in a
different register. Take both, registers I mean, and sing.

Friends, Birds and Wind

The gusts come out of nowhere.
The gist too.
The pelicans are just there
in out or side-sailed with it
locked and stiff in buffeted flight
though it's the wind we call stiff.
My friend too has been into the wind
and me, flying against it.
Who is more comical
the pelican fighting its way north to breed
or the two men shivering
trying to hold binoculars steady
in the stuff out of nowhere
the uselessness of knowing
anything more than what's said
when the tattooed redneck
pops out of his truck
laughing and friendly
to tell us.

Notes from cranes

cranes flying in

a little disagreement
among the second violins

the whole sky is written!

First Performance of
John Cage's *4'33"*

The phone rings at 4'17".
My mom.

      ninety-two when she enters the performance.

Anodyne

pain's anodyne
it turns out:
to feel it

my pin number sleeps in the fetal position

across the street,
the willow-legged girl
speaks Portuguese

what happens: is

a bowl holds a wheatfield

Try not to force it

the wind is a river the pelican swims in

Flight

When beauty sits in the next seat,
you (meaning *I*) do not notice her
the length of the short flight
wrapped in her chrysalis jacket, asleep.

Only when plane touches runway
and she coughs, sniffles, unfurls
do you see. Her phone rings
the instant she turns it on.

I have it with me, she smiles.

And it's true: she always
has it with her, is exactly
an age, has someone who knows
exactly what he has.

And in the exacting world,
it is always a short flight to leave,
long to connect, locate
all the unseen and noticed gods.

Pyrex Dish

My parents were married sixty years. I'm single, though it's only felt that way the last two years. With time to spare after the breakup, I visit, helping my mother in the aftermath of Dad's illness and dying. I need to cool something in a bowl of water, and find a dish down in the bottom cupboard. It's a clear Pyrex casserole that's been in their kitchen since I was a kid. When I pick it up, it feels like their marriage. When I write the poem, I realize it's my lack of one.

> sixty years of marriage
> the pyrex dish so scratched
> it's translucent, moving to opaque
>
> still works fine
>
> they never did need to see through it

Things To Do in a Free Country

Fire is thinking of all the ways people cry
her name, how a line of thought can change
the way twists and turns occur in a life.
Fire is making something here about the edge of a shriek
that's always there these days, as if
the heat could rise in dried out walls, as if
the smoke could know each unfortunate door
and knock politely, then find the children first,
as if this figure told the future, the cities
burning like so many metaphors, as if
it were in fact too late. Is it? There is
no smoke, no fire, just a man slumped in a chair
watching his country invade the world on t.v.
He knows the levers of power are not so easy
as buttons on the remote. He watches as we bring
weapons of every degree of destruction
as if to please each hour's primary target audience.
But he is thinking of all the ways people cry
as we burn them until they are free
to do what we do: turn off the t.v., put down the remote,
scream all you want to.

Dear Letter

Thank you for your brave letter. I've slept with it these two nights, variously treasuring, wrinkling and holding it . . .

Although you haven't written, I am still holding it, as you can see.

My friend the letter S. once read Camus' *The Stranger* on a plane returning from Europe. Later, she couldn't remember the name of the book, but told me how she had lost her ground, reading it. How she felt as if the desert light from Camus had gone right through her, as if she wasn't there. Somewhere in her feelings I remembered the book.

She wanted to know if I thought she would be okay.

I don't know, S., I hold your wrinkled, brave letter, too.

As if I were myself transparent. The truth is, the poem is not addressed to the letter S. Dear Letter, truth is, I have not lost your brave letter, though it was difficult to read and you haven't written it.

One theory is we do not write letters any more because letters require a sense of absence. In the same way that love requires a sense of loss to be full, the written word sealed in an envelope makes sense of the world as physical space, traversed by foot or hoof, wheel or wing, to bring the actual object, in an unsure and distant future, into the hands of the deared one, as if to stain the other with ink, indelibly. Most art tries to do this, but letters, as correspondence, enact it physically across space and time.

I read *The Stranger*, twice, in college. But I didn't get it, not really, till S. told me the story of a nameless book she had read on the flight from Europe. About losing her ground. Somewhere in her feelings I understood the book.

If time is a large room, and the objects in it always present, then we move through time to be present to ourselves. To the objects in us. *Things do not connect*, Jack Spicer once wrote, *they correspond*.

Dear Letter, I am writing you here to hold and wrinkle. Somewhere in your feelings I understand the book.

Invisible Man

you slip into the break and look around writes elision invisibly

(pages 12 to 13 are not shown in this preview)

elision a stand-in for ellison   for

the interstitial space between letters   space   the mind erases

  in reading
                        for the letters themselves, erased to see words
the words
erased for ideas ideas   *I expect to see values blossom* writes
williams

     and now it is a tree in spring   it is

the interstitial space in this erasing   you drop down into
   like Louis Armstrong in Ralph Ellison
the only elision
          the invisibility of well lit basements

    yet the mouth at the podium   its conspicuous space

  (the *it* a malleable figure the preposition a verb the hand a way of
hearing the word the gaps
between raised dots of finger-read braille   gaps that make
           the world signify)

   you slip into the break and look around writes ellison invisibly

as elision everywhere writes visibly

mi dónde

the aztec air of *huitzil* colonial eeee of *colibrí*
zun zun tentenelaire *zit zit* huitzil colibrí tiny
hummingword *zut zut* Zurita's sky-written bird
stutter me a little enjambment in raspy squeak
click onomatopoiesis, right me the typeface
makes car look like ear for you are my vehicle
today

Eastern Kingbird at Cardinals Game

The flies the so-called tyrant
flycatcher catches
back of home,
his weird drop-flight
not-glide flutter-hover,
his perch the cable
holds up the mesh
behind home plate
so we can sit there safe
and attend to the game
to all its ways of noticing
things, the way
for instance, grid and bird
disappear
at the crack of a bat
the way my friend says
maple sounds the best the
way the kingbird feeds
insouciant, oblivious
to 35,009 (announced)
the way one suddenly notices
the lights are on in the 4th
or wonders what a bird attends to
(there, his non-swoop drop flight)
is it all bugs and territory?
It's hard not to think
of him as the performer
taking a last turn

at the top of the sixth
(though we don't know that yet)
his catch, catch float twirl
rise, as Schumacher doubles
and the pinch hitter, a kid
named Hamilton, bloops
one in so Theriot
can bring them home
in the deep dusk
when the bird is gone
to some roost I suppose,
still musing, as the game
diminishes into the ninth,
when the closer leads with a first-pitch change
like putting the turn at the top of a sonnet.

The prompt was

unparaphrasable except as this poem
      or a squished rubber toy
      a curse
      a word prison
a list of homonyms for the word no   [*no no no no nooo!*]
        one of them spelled
          n-o-h for the noh theatre of japan
            yet no one can know which word is noh
or maybe the prompt was paraphrasable as
          I don't know . . . contrails?
      the way the sky does its slow erase
         of everything
        outside the brackets.
Maybe the prompt was the brackets.
I don't know. What do you think?

los zumbidos y susurros

plumas for Jami
short is fine, long is fine

during the week, the rooster will be incessant

you will write
                    dreams on the backs of your poems at night
it will be reassuring that poems have backs

        you will stumble over
                        the polvito orgásmica
                            in Salcedo
            the veil of needles
in Vicuña   you will get the names backward
            mistakes will be important

            it will be consoling to have these women in your poem

what they know of the thread that is water   or the ways of
            the body threaded down into ground

you will trick yourself into a little courage
and the rooster will be incessant

los zumbidos y susurros will only refer to hummingbirds
their plumas you have tried to write on

For the Moment in a World Where the Bird

I would change all the marks that adorn you. Rename them. Your eyebrows, for instance, would be girls-woken-by-birds-at-3-a.m., and in speaking to you, who is pretty much the least supercilious person I've known, I'd say things like "don't raise your girls-woken-by-birds-at-3-a.m.'s at me," in fact, don't raise them at all, and here I'm not quoting, just thinking out loud, how the need to rename things is just another attempt to beat back fear. The truth is I wake up pretty scared most nights, though, you know, it's only *scared of myself*. Honestly, I think that fear is a terribly under-recognized emotional grouping, especially in the sphere of so-called love, but that belongs in a different poem. Yes, this is a poem, though it lacks official line breaks, which serve as a kind of fake punctuation for those whose side lost the war, or those who aren't even aware of the war because they weren't there in one way or another, but that is another essay. Yes, this is an essay, though it doesn't have official paragraphs, renames punctuation, calls Howard Nemerov an old fart bag and even feels dubious about Donald Finkel, though it counts him as a friend, being aware as it is that a number of one's friends can be baggy at times, which goes for me too, and now the poem is a short story. I wrote it for the moment in a world where the bird really does sing at 3 a.m., and all the forms we argue and fret about are only punctuation in the end.

Breaks in Small Places

syllable   unit of sounding   unit of breaking   ontological fields

    breaking
       the space a
  heart sits in

      syllable
         your word is a body
           that breaks in small places

                  therefore *latch* therefore
join

       the syllable, which holds the body together, is
       pronounced with a single un
interrupted sounding of the voice
         this unit of breaking / unit of sounding
     the voice I am latched to
          voices I am joined with

like yours

       we live in the break   in the un and the
       interrupted

    sounding   of speech

in a heart, in
  a voice, remembered

—for Jane Mead

Page

The page is a small measure, the paragraph its whirring space, here
in a field of hummingbirds near Point Reyes, California. Ten, fifteen
hummers working the flowered sedge, you can see this because the
page is a flip-card animation in front of every other page, (you or I
or we) have experienced, which is what's so convenient about the flat
plane its pail a small measure of the milk the water the acid the flour
the rocks it might hold. Here, I have made bright watercolor-like
abstract markings in black and white, whirrrrrr, the hummingbirds
working the sedge, whirrrrrr, the flip-card animation working the
page held in front of the other field of perception near Point Reyes,
California, moved up and across, or down and back, across, or back
and forth, the way everything changes. I am doing this all day,
thinking of different things. When the attempted allegory breaks
into plane, the hummingbirds burst out onto page.

nebraska

diesel chitchat gear hell
back-weep back-weep back-weep
dot dot dit dit dot dit mallet
hey hey wood in mall-et hey hey
hey hey saw sear s saws sawdust
at the tree shore here
o o o nailgun go
bram bram bram lintel in
gonk gonk gonk gonk on sill
dink dink dink on dowel in
hey - hey hey - hey hey
hey
next door! you-you
you-you back-weep dot
dit s saw o go slam
ding bam dunk
new shift
don't stop
no no hey! hey! hey!
work crew
not through
hey!
we're building a poem

Listening to Epistrophy
on the Great Plains

From late February to early April, over 600,000 sandhill cranes
converge on the Platte River in Nebraska.

—visitkearney.org

epistrophy that great location in the monk coltrane recordings we

start exactly there, reading destinations at a distance, the version
where horn and reed take the opening spiral the keyboard usually
plays

the fields are crane repeat coltrane filled cranefield horn fill monk
offed halt

                stammer
the plain jumpovers and austere stubble the almost tender crane
gargle trill music

reading the destinations   at a distance   passing middle age

we are alone

        (I   is   an   other)

   and age:

   is a thousand voices in the wakened field

The Difference Between Crows and Ravens in Missouri

Crows are big, but ravens are enormous, roughly the size of
a red-tailed hawk. Crows don't mind the city, while ravens,
they're more cautious on the whole. The raven's name is derived
from the Old Norse echoic *hrafn*, meaning *to clear one's throat*,
and crow, though similarly echoic—from the Old High
German *kra* and Old English *crawe*—seems to have gotten
conflated, somewhere along the line, with roosters at dawn.

Pema Chödrön, American Tibetan Buddhist, born Deirdre,
describes how in the gale-winter winds off Cape Breton,
Nova Scotia, ravens grip the trees first with their claws,
then beaks too, till finally letting go, *wheeeee*, into the wind.
And back again. In case you haven't noticed, the crow flies
in a straight line, while ravens proceed by indirection.

The form of a raven's mind is akin to that of a big Danish loogie
hockered expertly downwind off the prow of a Viking ship right
after someone *hrafned*, which is why we need strange creatures
to live amongst us in our all too human world. Our languages go
back to a time when birds were named, when minds happened on
the place where first things were attached to first sounds, before
the great dilution that makes a language, its endless conventions
singing amongst themselves. Poetry tries to return to that earlier
state, the poem a big onomatopoetic blurting. *Ach-oo. Gesundheit.*

Crows fly in a straight line, ravens proceed by indirection, as we've
seen. Software engineers write code to leverage a prefabricated
computer chip so a line of processing falls through it, sort of like a
pachinko machine with a ball dropping through its gates, sorting,

sorting, if-then-else, that's all it is, yet people, cawing loudly from the tops of trees, have come to believe that this is thinking.

Metaphor latches onto the dominant mode, modes of its time. The poem was once a machine made of words; now the computer is a machine running a machine made of words, which has as little to do with poetry as the execution of code has to do with thinking. The computer, like the raven, is filled with intelligence. But only one of them can think.

Ravens are not engineers. Snyder describes one *on a roost of furs, no bird in a bird book, black as the sun.* Ravens have been observed working with wolf packs, leading them to prey. A raven's beak cannot pierce hide, therefore they feed through the eyes or rely on vultures, other predatory mammals, cars, humans, flesh tearers and cutters.

Ravens don't exist in Missouri. They are gliders, soarers, no pedestrian flappers. I wrote this for Richard, who asked me the difference between crows and ravens in Missouri.

> john cage was an expert in mycology
> sappho wrote in another century
> why is everything an invocation now?
>
> o whack-eyed comedian, radiant
> and gleaming phlegm-throated liar
> speak, become as voice to me
>
> o four fingered wing of gale-loosened
> flight, cave-drawn corvid independent
> of tree to frame your perching
>
> o thieving, mean spirited self
> server who helps only to eat

or breed, give me your morphemes

o velar \ k \ of *cool*, palatal of *keel*
the distance from kill to kiss
a single phoneme, teach me how

to stammer, hiccup, hocker, sing
o I-feeding speaker for the eating
of your tribe, for the lost, the thief,

the once stolen life in the lied-to mind

Acknowledgments

Cimarron Review: "Things To Do in a Free Country"

Denver Quarterly: "'Mourning, Morning,' I say" · "Placement of the No's"

Kenyon Review: "Egrets, Regrets"

Lana Turner: "Invisible Man" · "[to say dehiscence]" · "Romance Sonámbulo" · "Listening to Epistrophy on the Great Plains"

Ninth Letter: "Translation Zone" (originally published as "Some Walls Are Doors For Creatures to Pass Through Between Shores")

Plume Poetry 9: "Plains"

Spillway: "An Introduction to the *Field Guide of North American Lycanthropy*"

UCityReview: "Anodyne" · "Dear Letter" · "Eastern Kingbird at Cardinals Game" · "Flight" · "Pyrex Dish"

VOLT: "Preliminary Remarks with Love Poem & Marriage Proposal" · "formal poem" · "Hummingbird Migration"

About the Author

Brian Cochran lives in University City, Missouri, a few miles south of where the Missouri and Mississippi rivers collide. He has received fellowships, residencies, and grants from the Millay Colony for the Arts, Bread Loaf, the Kimmel Harding Nelson Center for the Arts, the Vermont Studio Center, and MacDowell. Brian has an M.F.A. from Washington University, and works as a writer at a small engineering firm in St. Louis.

Gratitude

For Cintia Santana, unwitting co-founder of the Sergio González Rodríguez School of Poetics, always.

For Sai, indelible ink, invisibly.

For my brother Kevin, now magical in un-magician-like ways.

For my brother Doug, for all his support from Chicago.

For my sister Barbara, always in the arts.

For hugs from Charles and Jay.

For the Wednesday Night Poets, Andy and Gene.

For David Baker, teacher and mentor.

For Thomas Fink, John Yau, and Sandy McIntosh, who made this book possible.

For Brenda Hillman, for what you've done in the world of poetry.

For Carrie in Missouri.

For the Community of Writers under a different name.

For the will to begin again.

Titles From Marsh Hawk Press

Jane Augustine *Arbor Vitae; Krazy; Night Lights; A Woman's Guide to Mountain Climbing*

Tom Beckett *Dipstick (Diptych)*

William Benton *Light on Water*

Sigman Byrd *Under the Wanderer's Star*

Patricia Carlin: *Original Green; Quantum Jitters; Second Nature*

Claudia Carlson *The Elephant House; My Chocolate Sarcophagus; Pocket Park*

Lorna Dee Cervantes: *April on Olympia*

Meredith Cole *Miniatures*

Jon Curley *Hybrid Moments; Scorch Marks; Remnant Halo*

Joanne D. Dwyer *RASA*

Neil de la Flor *Almost Dorothy; An Elephant's Memory of Blizzards*

Chard deNiord *Sharp Golden Thorn*

Sharon Dolin *Serious Pink*

Joanne Dominique Dwyer *Rasa*

Steve Fellner *Blind Date with Cavafy; The Weary World Rejoices*

Thomas Fink *Zeugma, Selected Poems & Poetic Series; Joyride; Peace Conference; Clarity and Other Poems; After Taxes; Gossip*

Thomas Fink and Maya D. Mason *A Pageant for Every Addiction*

Norman Finkelstein *Inside the Ghost Factory; Passing Over*

Edward Foster *A Looking-Glass for Traytors; The Beginning of Sorrows; Dire Straits; Mahrem: Things Men Should Do for Men; Sewing the Wind; What He Ought to Know*

Paolo Javier *The Feeling is Actual*

Burt Kimmelman *Abandoned Angel; Somehow; Steeple at Sunrise; Zero Point Poiesis; with Fred Caruso The Pond at Cape May Point*

Basil King *Disparate Beasts: Basil King's Beastiary, Part Two; 77 Beasts; Disparate Beasts; Mirage; The Spoken Word / The Painted Hand from Learning to Draw / A History*

Martha King *Imperfect Fit*

Phillip Lopate *At the End of the Day*

Mary Mackey *Breaking the Fever; The Jaguars That Prowl Our Dreams; Sugar Zone; Travelers With No Ticket Home; Creativity*

Jason McCall *Dear Hero*

Sandy McIntosh *The After-Death History of My Mother; Between Earth and Sky; Cemetery Chess; Ernesta, in the Style of the Flamenco; Forty-Nine Guaranteed Ways to Escape Death; A Hole In the Ocean; Lesser Lights; Obsessional; Plan B: A Poet's Survivors Manual*

Stephen Paul Miller *Any Lie You Tell Will Be the Truth; The Bee Flies in May; Fort Dad; Skinny Eighth Avenue; There's Only One God and You're Not It*

Daniel Morris *Blue Poles; Bryce Passage; Hit Play; If Not for the Courage*

Gail Newman *Blood Memory*

Geoffrey O'Brien *Where Did Poetry Come From; The Blue Hill*

Sharon Olinka *The Good City*

Christina Olivares *No Map of the Earth Includes Stars*

Justin Petropoulos *Eminent Domain*

Paul Pines *Charlotte Songs; Divine Madness; Gathering Sparks; Last Call at the Tin Palace*

Jacquelyn Pope *Watermark*

George Quasha *Things Done for Themselves*

Karin Randolph *Either She Was*

Rochelle Ratner *Balancing Acts; Ben Casey Days; House and Home*

Michael Rerick *In Ways Impossible to Fold*

Corrine Robins *Facing It; One Thousand Years; Today's Menu*

Eileen R. Tabios *Because I love you I Become War; The Connoisseur of Alleys; I Take Thee, English, for My Beloved; The In(ter)vention of the Hay(na)ku; The Light Sang as It Left Your Eyes; Reproductions of the Empty Flagpole; Sun Stigmata; The Thorn Rosary*

Eileen R. Tabios and j/j hastain *The Relational Elations of Orphaned Algebra*

Tony Trigilio: *Proof Something Happened; Craft: a Memoir*

Susan Terris *Familiar Tense; Ghost of Yesterday; Natural Defenses; On Becoming a Poet* (editor)

Lynne Thompson *Fretwork*

Madeline Tiger *Birds of Sorrow and Joy*

Tana Jean Welch *Latest Volcano*

Harriet Zinnes: *Drawing on the Wall; Light Light or the Curvature of the Earth; New and Selected Poems; Weather is Whether; Whither Nonstopping*

YEAR	AUTHOR	TITLE	JUDGE
2004	Jacquelyn Pope	*Watermark*	Marie Ponsot
2005	Sigman Byrd	*Under the Wanderer's Star*	Gerald Stern
2006	Steve Fellner	*Blind Date with Cavafy*	Denise Duhamel
2007	Karin Randolph	*Either She Was*	David Shapiro
2008	Michael Rerick	*In Ways Impossible to Fold*	Thylias Moss
2009	Neil de la Flor	*Almost Dorothy*	Forrest Gander
2010	Justin Petropoulos	*Eminent Domain*	Anne Waldman
2011	Meredith Cole	*Miniatures*	Alicia Ostriker
2012	Jason McCall	*Dear Hero,*	Cornelius Eady
2013	Tom Beckett	*Dipstick (Diptych)*	Charles Bernstein
2014	Christina Olivares	*No Map of the Earth Includes Stars*	Brenda Hillman
2015	Tana Jean Welch	*Latest Volcano*	Stephanie Strickland
2016	Robert Gibb	*After*	Mark Doty
2017	Geoffrey O'Brien	*The Blue Hill*	Meena Alexander
2018	Lynne Thompson	*Fretwork*	Jane Hirshfield
2019	Gail Newman	*Blood Memory*	Marge Piercy
2020	Tony Trigilio	*Proof Something Happened*	Susan Howe
2021	Joanne D. Dwyer	*Rasa*	David Lehman
2022	Brian Cochran	*Translation Zone*	John Yau